Silly, Silly Mary

Written by PATRICIA DEMPSEY

Illustrated by MELINDA WOLFE

To order additional copies of this book, contact:
Xlibris
1-888-795-4274
www.Xlibris.com
Orders@Xlibris.com

Library of Congress Control Number: 2011928502

ISBN: Hardcover   978-1-4653-3542-6
            Softcover   978-1-4653-3543-3

Library of Congress Control Number:

To Mari,
You were the inspiration for this story.

To Mary,
You are so silly.
—P.D.

To my parents, grandmother and Eric
You color my world with love.
—M.W.

Silly, Silly Mary,
Loves to play all day.
Today she has asked,
Some friends to come and stay.

Mary took out paints,
And lots of crayons, too.
Everyone got to work,
Some painted, some drew.

9

Silly, Silly Mary,
She loves the color RED.
She painted this picture,
Of a silly monster head.

Mary has a buddy,
Her name is Carolee.
She likes the color YELLOW,
And draws a bumble bee.

Along comes Frankie,
His favorite color is BLUE.
He gets to work,
And draws a big canoe.

Then there is Timmy,
He likes the color GREEN.
He made the cutest frog,
That Mary's ever seen!

Trudy loves ORANGE and says,
"It's the best color for me!"
She paints an orange boat,
floating in the sea.

Here comes Carly,
She loves the color PURPLE.
She paints slow and steady,
And makes the perfect circle.

Next to draw is Molly,
She loves the color PINK.
Her drawing shows a picture
Of a pig that likes to wink!

Then comes Billy,
He likes the color **BROWN**.
He painted a clown,
Whose pants fell down!

Sally is ready,
She likes the color WHITE.
She draws a face,
With a smile that is bright.

Finally there is Zack,
He likes the color **BLACK**.
He shows off his picture,
Of his cute dog Mack.

Mary was so happy,
She had a busy day.
She loves all her friends,
And wanted them to stay.

When her friends went home,
She hung the pictures to dry.
And would give them back to them,
The next time they came by.

Silly, Silly Mary

Printed in the United States
By Bookmasters